# RECIPES FROM
# GRANNY'S KITCHEN

# Books of similar interest from Random House Value Publishing:

Amish Cooking

As American As Apple Pie

Christmas Memories with Recipes

Pennsylvania Dutch Cooking

The Pioneer Lady's Country Christmas

# RECIPES FROM GRANNY'S KITCHEN

## Helen Jenkins

Gramercy Books
New York

This 2000 edition is published by Gramercy Books™, an imprint of Random House Value Publishing, Inc., 201 East 50th Street, New York, N.Y. 10022

Gramercy Books™ and design are trademarks of Random House Value Publishing, Inc.

Random House
New York • Toronto • London • Sydney • Auckland
http://www.randomhouse.com/

Design by Robert Yaffe

Printed and bound in the United States of America.

**Library of Congress Cataloging—in—Publication Data**

Jenkins, Helen, 1932–
    Recipes from granny's kitchen / Helen Jenkins.
        p    cm.
    ISBN 0-517-20685-4 (hardcover)
    1. Cookery, American.    I. Title.
    TX715 .J528  2000
    641.5973--dc21                                        99-43594
                                                                         CIP

9 8 7 6 5 4 3 2 1

# Contents

## Side Dishes and Salads . . . . . . . . . . . . 45

Sweet Potato Pie

Pan-Roasted Potatoes

Creamy Mashed Potatoes

Basic Bread Stuffing

Buttercup Squash

Sweet Noodle Pudding

Boston Baked Beans

Corn Pudding

Tomato Onion Bake

Roasted Asparagus with Lemon

Ratatouille

Creamed Spinach

Orange Rice

Spinach Salad

Lentil Salad with Balsamic Vinaigrette

Blue Cheese Salad Dressing

Italian Salad Dressing

Barbecue Sauce

Triple-Cranberry Sauce

Fried Apple Rings

## Desserts . . . . . . . . . . . . . . . . . . . . . 55

Phoebe's Pound Cake

Pecan Squares

Black Forest Cherry Cake

Carrot Cake

Elegant Poached Pears

All-American Apple Pie

Grammy Wendy's Christmas Cookies

Peach Cobbler

Strawberry Buttermilk Biscuit
   Shortcake

Mud Pie

Lemon Squares

Rice Pudding

Chocolate Chip Cheesecake

Lemon Meringue Pie

Key Lime Pie

# Breakfast and Brunch

# American Country Biscuits

1 package dry yeast
1/2 cup warm water
5 cups flour
4 tsp baking powder
2 tsp salt
3 Tbsp sugar
3/4 cup shortening
1 tsp baking soda
2 cups buttermilk

In a small bowl, sprinkle yeast over the water, stir, and let stand 5 minutes to dissolve. In a large mixing bowl, combine the flour, baking powder, salt, and sugar. Stir with a fork to mix. Add the shortening and cut into the flour mixture, either using your fingertips or a pastry cutter, until the mixture looks crumbly.

Add the baking soda to the buttermilk. Stir the buttermilk into the flour mixture. Add the yeast mixture and blend well. Cover and refrigerate for about 8 hours.

Turn the dough onto a lightly floured board. Knead a dozen times. Roll out dough to about 1/2-inch thickness. Cut out the biscuits with a 2-inch cutter and place them 1 inch apart on greased baking pans. Cover and let rise for 1 hour.

Preheat oven to 400°F and bake for about 15 minutes, or until lightly browned. Serve hot.

# Citrusy French Toast

6 large eggs
1/2 cup orange juice
1/3 cup milk
1-1/2 Tbsp packed brown sugar
1/4 tsp freshly grated nutmeg
8 slices whole-wheat bread
butter for frying (approx 1-1/2 Tbsp)
Confectioners' sugar
Warm maple syrup

Preheat oven to 250°F.

In a shallow baking dish, whisk together eggs, orange juice, milk, brown sugar and nutmeg. Add 4 bread slices and soak 2 minutes. Turn slices over and soak 2 more minutes. Remove bread slices to a plate and soak the remaining 4 bread slices.

In a large, heavy skillet, heat the butter over moderate heat. Cook half the bread slices until golden. Transfer French toast to a baking sheet and keep warm in oven. Prepare the remaining slices in the same way. Dust with confectioners' sugar and serve with syrup.

*Lorraine Gordon, now a grandmother herself, remembers her grandmother making this whenever she came up from Florida to Pennsylvania for a spring visit.*

# Hot Cross Buns

*This Easter recipe comes from Lorraine Dunn's large family in Springfield, Missouri, but she serves these buns all year 'round.*

1-1/2 cups milk
1/4 cup shortening
1 tsp yeast
6 Tbsp sugar + 1 tsp sugar
1/2 tsp salt
1 egg, lightly beaten
6 cups flour

1 tsp cinnamon
1/3 cup raisins
1/3 cup currants

Glaze:
1 cup confectioners' sugar
1 Tbsp hot water

Scald milk, shortening and sugar; cool to lukewarm. Mash yeast with sugar, add to milk. Add currants and raisins. Sift flour, salt and cinnamon and add to mixture to form dough.

Turn out onto a lightly floured board and knead the dough until smooth and elastic. Put into a greased bowl, cover, and let rise in a warm place until very light.

Divide dough into rounds a little larger than biscuits, work each round into a smooth ball and place on greased baking pan 1 inch apart. Place the buns 1-inch apart on the sheets. Let the buns rise again until light, about 1 hour.

Preheat the oven to 375°F. Bake for approximately 20 minutes, or until the buns are golden on top. Remove and make glaze by combining confectioners' sugar and water until medium thick. Apply the glaze with a toothpick or pastry bag, forming the shape of a cross on top of each bun.

# Banana Oatmeal Waffles

1-1/4 cups flour
3/4 cup regular oats (not instant), uncooked
3 Tbsp brown sugar
1 Tbsp baking powder
1/2 tsp baking soda
1/4 tsp ground cinnamon
Pinch of ground nutmeg
1-1/2 cups buttermilk
2 large eggs
1/4 cup butter, melted
2 medium bananas, chopped

Mix all ingredients except bananas until smooth. Add bananas and mix to blend. Bake in preheated waffle iron until golden. Top with fresh strawberries if desired. This recipe can also be used to make pancakes.

# Cranberry Muffins

2 cups flour
4 Tbsp sugar
1 Tbsp baking powder
1/2 teaspoon salt
2 eggs, well beaten
1 cup warm milk
1/4 lb butter, melted and cooled slightly
1 cup fresh cranberries

Preheat oven to 400°F. Sift flour, 4 tablespoons sugar, baking
powder, and salt together. Stir 3/4 cup chopped cranberries with
1/4 cup sugar and add to dry mixture. Combine the eggs, milk, and
butter and add to mixture, stirring only until moist. Spoon into
well-greased muffin tins. Bake approximately 20 minutes or until
toothpick inserted in top comes out clean. Serve immediately. You
may substitute blueberries for the cranberries.

# Breakfast-to-Last-
# All-Day Casserole

8 slices white bread, cut into cubes
1 pound bulk pork sausage, crumbled and cooked
1-1/2 cups grated sharp cheddar cheese
10 large eggs
2 cups whole milk
2 tsp dry mustard
1 tsp salt
Pepper
Butter to grease pan

Preheat oven to 350°F. Grease 9 x 13-inch glass baking dish. Place bread in prepared dish.
    Top with sausage and cheese. Beat together eggs and next three ingredients.
Season with pepper. Pour over sausage mixture.
    Bake casserole until puffed and center is set, about 50 minutes. Cut into
squares.

# Oatmeal Raisin Scones

4 cups flour
1/3 cup sugar
1-3/4 tsp baking powder
1 tsp baking soda
1 tsp salt
1/2 lb (2 sticks) butter, chilled
3 cups rolled oats
1 cup raisins
2 cups buttermilk

Preheat oven to 375° F. In a large bowl, mix together flour, sugar, baking powder, baking soda, and salt. Cut the cold butter into small pieces and add to the flour mixture. Use your fingers or a pastry cutter to cut the butter into the flour until the mixture resembles coarse crumbs. Add the oats and raisins, tossing or stirring with a fork to distribute evenly. Add the buttermilk and stir with a fork until you can gather the dough into a rough ball.

   Sprinkle a board with flour and put the dough on it. Knead 6 or 7 times. Divide the dough into 3 equal parts. Pat each part into a circle about /2-inch thick. Cut each circle into 10 wedges. Put the wedges on ungreased baking sheets about 1/2 inch apart. Bake for about 25 minutes, or until the scones are lightly brown. Serve warm.

# Scotch Eggs

1 1/4 pounds bulk country-style or herbed sausage
1 tsp crumbled dried sage
1/2 tsp dried thyme, crumbled
1/4 tsp cayenne
4 hard-boiled large eggs
1/2 cup all-purpose flour
2 raw large eggs, beaten lightly
1 cup fresh bread crumbs
Vegetable oil for deep-frying the eggs

In a large bowl combine the sausage, the sage, the thyme, and the cayenne.
Divide the mixture into 4 equal portions, and flatten each portion into a thin
patty. Enclose each hard-boiled egg completely in 1 of the patties, forming a
round.

Dredge the sausage-coated eggs in the flour, shaking off the excess, dip them
in the raw eggs, letting the excess drip off, and roll them gently in the bread
crumbs, coating them well.

In a deep frying pan heat 2 1/2 inches of
the oil to 350°F. and in it fry the Scotch eggs, 2
at a time for about 10 minutes, turning them
and transferring them to paper towels to
drain as they are done.

# Scalloped Eggs

1/4 lb (1 stick) butter
3 cups bread crumbs
8 hard-boiled eggs, sliced
Salt and pepper to taste
1/2 tsp grated nutmeg
1-1/2 cups milk

Preheat oven to 400°F. Butter a round, shallow baking dish or a 9-inch round
glass pie plate.

Melt the butter in a large skillet. Add the crumbs and cook over low heat,
stirring often until the crumbs are golden and have absorbed the butter.

Spread half the crumbs evenly over the bottom of the baking dish. Arrange
egg slices over the crumbs. Sprinkle with salt, pepper, and half the nutmeg. Pour
the milk over the egg slices and spread the remaining crumbs evenly over the
top. Dust the top with nutmeg. Bake for about 25 minutes and serve hot.

# Baked Eggs in Pastry with Herbs

*When I spent the weekend at my grandmother's house near Saratoga Springs, New York, she would always serve this for Sunday breakfast. With baked fruit on the side, this was quite a meal.*
        *-Toinette Carlin*

4 prepared tart crust shells
1/4 cup (1 oz) shredded provolone, Muenster or similar
    semisoft medium-aged cheese
2 tsp mixed chopped fresh herbs such as tarragon, chives,
    chervil, thyme and/or flat-leaf (Italian) parsley, in any combination
8 large eggs
2 Tbsp unsalted butter, cut into bits
4 Tbsp (2 fl oz) heavy cream

Preheat oven to 350°F. Pre-cook tart shells if indicated.
    Sprinkle about 1 teaspoon of the cheese into the bottom of each pastry shell. In a small dish, stir together the remaining cheese and the herbs. Break 2 eggs into each pastry shell, positioning them around the bottom, and dot the tops with the butter, dividing it equally. Sprinkle the cheese-herb mixture evenly over the tops, then spoon 1 tablespoon of cream on top of each tart
    Bake until the eggs have set, about 8 minutes. Remove from the oven and let cool for 1 minute. Using a narrow spatula, carefully transfer to warmed individual plates and serve immediately.

# Ham 'n' Egg Roll-Ups

8 large eggs
1/3 cup light cream
2 Tbsp finely chopped fresh parsley or 2 tsp dried parsley
1/2 tsp fines herbes
Salt and pepper to taste
2–3 Tbsp butter
4 oz cream cheese, cut into little pieces
8 slices of cooked ham

Whisk together eggs, cream, parsley, herbs, and salt and pepper in a bowl. Melt butter in large frying pan and pour in egg mixture. Scramble over medium-low heat until just set. Stir in cream cheese and then remove eggs from heat.
    Lay ham slices flat. Place a portion of eggs onto each slice and then roll up. Hold together with toothpicks and serve.

# Cranberry Nut Bread

4 cups flour
2 cups sugar
3 tsp baking powder
1 tsp baking soda
1 tsp salt
2 eggs beaten

Juice of 3 oranges
4 Tbsp melted butter
Boiling water
2 cups chopped walnuts
2 cups sliced cranberries

Preheat oven to 350°F. Butter and flour 2 loaf pans. In a large bowl, sift together flour, sugar, baking powder, baking soda and salt. Add eggs and stir. In a heat-proof measuring cup, combine the orange juice and melted butter, and then add enough boiling water to make 1-1/2 cups liquid. Add liquid to dough and mix well. Stir in walnuts and cranberries.

Pour batter into prepared pans and let sit on counter for 20 minutes. Then bake for 45–60 minutes until golden and a tester inserted in center comes out clean. Makes 2 loaves.

# Popovers

1 cup sifted flour
1/2 tsp salt
2 large eggs
1 cup milk
Melted butter for brushing pan

Preheat oven to 450°F. Sift flour and salt together into a large bowl. In a small bowl, whisk together the eggs and milk. Add milk mixture to the flour and stir the batter until it is smooth.

In the preheated oven, heat a six-cup popover pan or muffin tin for 5 minutes until hot. Brush the cups with the melted butter, and fill them halfway with the batter. Fill any empty cups with water to avoid burning. Bake in the middle of the oven for 20 minutes; reduce the heat to 375°F and bake popovers for another 20 minutes until they are golden brown and crisp. Prick them to let steam out before serving.

# Vermont Cheddar and Apple Pancake

According to my grandma Lucy, this is good any time of the year, but especially in the fall when the air and the apples are at their crispiest.

-Gina Cummings

1/3 cup + 2 Tbsp flour
2 Tbsp sugar
2/3 cup milk
2 large eggs
Pinch of salt
3/4 cup shredded sharp Cheddar cheese
1 small tart apple, peeled, cored, and cut into thin wedges
1 Tbsp unsalted butter
Confectioners' sugar

Preheat oven to 375°F. Blend flour, 1 tablespoon sugar, milk, eggs, and salt in a food processor or medium-size bowl. Process or whisk until batter is smooth. Add the cheese and mix.

In a 10 to 12-inch ovenproof skillet, melt the butter over moderately high heat, coating the sides and bottom of pan. Add the apples and cook for 3 minutes, until the apple is tender and just beginning to brown. Sprinkle the remaining tablespoon of sugar over the apple. Remove from heat.

Spread the apple wedges evenly over the bottom of the pan. Pour the batter over the wedges. Bake uncovered for about 30 minutes or until the pancake is browned and puffy. Remove the pancake from the oven and sprinkle with confectioners' sugar. Cut in wedges to serve.

# Bayou Breakfast Puffs

1/3 cup shortening
1/2 cup sugar
1 egg
1-1/2 cups flour
1-1/2 tsp baking powder
1/2 tsp salt
1/4 tsp ground nutmeg
1/2 cup milk
1/2 cup sugar
1 teaspoon ground cinnamon
1/4 lb (1 stick) butter or margarine, melted

Preheat oven to 350°F. Grease 12-cup muffin tin.

In a large bowl, mix shortening, 1/2 cup sugar and the egg thoroughly. Stir in flour, baking powder, salt and nutmeg alternately with milk. Divide batter evenly among muffin cups. Bake 20–25 minutes or until golden brown.

Mix 1/2 cup sugar and the cinnamon. Roll hot muffins immediately in melted butter or margarine, then in sugar-cinnamon mixture. Serve hot. Makes 15 puffs.

# Blueberry Coffee Cake

1/4 cup salad oil
1 beaten egg
1/2 cup milk
1 1/2 cups sifted all-purpose flour
3/4 cup sugar
2 tsp baking powder
1/2 tsp salt

For topping:
1/3 cup brown sugar
1 tablespoon all-purpose flour
1 teaspoon ground cinnamon
1/2 cup broken walnuts
1 Tbsp melted butter
3/4 cup fresh or thawed frozen blueberries

Preheat oven to 375°F.

In a bowl, combine salad oil, egg, and milk. Sift together dry ingredients and add them to the milk mixture. Mix well. In another bowl, combine all ingredients for topping.

Pour cake batter into a greased 9 x 9 x 2-inch pan. Spread blueberries evenly over batter. Top that with the cinnamon nut mixture. Bake for 25–30 minutes. Serves 6 to 12.

# Blueberry Johnnycakes with Maple Syrup

2 cups yellow cornmeal
1 cup flour
1/2 cup sugar
1 Tbsp baking powder
3/4 tsp salt
1/4 lb (1 stick) chilled butter, diced
1-1/2 cups milk
3 large eggs
2 cups fresh blueberries or frozen blueberries, unthawed
Warm maple syrup

Preheat oven to 400°F. Butter bottom of 13 x 9 x 2 baking pan. Mix first 5 ingredients in food processor. Add butter and cut in, using on/off turns, until mixture resembles coarse meal. Beat milk and eggs in large bowl to blend. Stir in cornmeal mixture. Mix in blueberries.

Transfer batter into prepared baking pan. Bake about 25 minutes, or until tester inserted into the center of corn bread comes out clean. Cut into large squares and serve warm with maple syrup.

# Sticky Buns

2 loaves frozen bread dough, thawed
1/2 cup (1 stick) margarine or butter
2 Tbsp sugar and cinnamon mixed
2 Tbsp milk
1 cup brown sugar
1 large box vanilla pudding (do not use instant)
1/2 cup raisins
1/2 cup pecans or chopped nuts

Grease a 9 x 13 inch pan. Place nuts and raisins on bottom, cut or tear one loaf of bread into pieces and place on nuts. Sprinkle with cinnamon-sugar mixture. In a medium-sized saucepan, melt one stick butter; add milk and brown sugar. Mix well. Add pudding and mix. Spread pudding mixture on bread in pan. Tear or cut remaining bread and place in empty spaces. Cover with towel and let rise (2 to 3 hours).

Preheat oven to 325°F. Bake at 325°F for 30–45 minutes. Remove from oven and immediately turn over onto platter. Cut apart buns when still warm.

# Soups

# Lentil Soup with Frankfurters

1 cup lentils
6 cups water
2 slices extra thick-sliced bacon, diced
1 leek or scallion, finely chopped
1 carrot, finely chopped
1 stalk celery, finely chopped
1 onion, finely chopped

1 Tbsp vegetable oil
2 Tbsp unbleached flour
1 Tbsp vinegar
4 frankfurters, thickly sliced
1 Tbsp ketchup
1 tsp salt
1/4 tsp black pepper

Wash the lentils thoroughly. In a 2 1/2-quart saucepan bring 6 cups of water to a boil. Add the lentils, bacon, leek or scallion, carrot and celery. Simmer, partially covered, for 30 to 40 minutes.

Meanwhile in a frying pan, sauté chopped onion in vegetable oil until soft. Sprinkle flour over onion, and stir. Lower heat, stir constantly, and cook until the flour turns a light brown. Be careful not to burn flour. Stir 1/2 cup of hot lentil soup into the browned flour; beat with a wire whisk until well-blended. Beat in vinegar.

Add contents of frying pan to soup in saucepan and stir together. Cover and simmer for 30 minutes or until lentils are soft. Add the frankfurters and ketchup. Cook to heat frankfurters through. Season with salt and pepper and serve hot. Serves 4.

# Black Bean Soup

1 lb (2 cups) dried black beans,
   soaked overnight
2-1/2 tsp salt
1/2 cup olive oil
1 large onion, chopped

1 large green pepper,
   seeded and chopped
6 cloves garlic, chopped
1-1/4 tsp dried oregano
1/4 tsp cayenne pepper
1/2 tsp black pepper

Drain the beans, and place them in a large pot. Add enough water to cover the beans by 1-1/2 inches and 1 teaspoon of the salt and cook over medium heat for 45 minutes.

Heat the olive oil in a large, heavy frying pan. Add the onion, green pepper, and garlic, and sauté until tender, about 3 minutes. Add the vegetables to the beans and then add the oregano, cayenne, black pepper, and remaining salt.

Simmer for 1 hour, adding more water if necessary. Taste for seasoning and serve.

# Clam Chowder

6 bacon slices, chopped
1-1/2 large onions, chopped
2 large (about 1-1/2 lbs) russet potatoes, peeled and cut into 1/2-inch pieces
1 large red pepper, chopped
3 10-oz cans baby clams, drained (reserve liquid)
2 cups whole milk
1/2 cup bottled clam juice
1 15-oz can cream-style corn
3 Tbsp chopped fresh thyme or 1 Tbsp dried
Salt and pepper to taste

Cook chopped bacon in heavy large saucepan over medium heat until fat is rendered and bacon begins to brown. Add onions and saute until tender, about 10 minutes. Add potatoes and red pepper and saute 1 minute. Add reserved liquid from clams, milk and clam juice and simmer uncovered about 15 minutes or until vegetables are tender.

   Add corn and clams to chowder and simmer until slightly thickened, about 5 minutes. Mix in chopped thyme. Season with salt and pepper.

*Sandy Catalbo remembers late August in Cape Cod, when the chilly air made this clam chowder as comforting as her grandmother's satin quilt.*

# Old-Fashioned Chicken Noodle Soup

*Every grandma's cure for the common cold. It always works.*

16 cups canned low-salt chicken broth
1 3 1/2-pound chicken, cut into 8 pieces
1/2 cup chopped onion
2 carrots, peeled, thinly sliced
2 celery stalks, sliced

2 Tbsp (1/4 stick) butter
1 cup sliced mushrooms
1 Tbsp fresh lemon juice
1 8-oz package wide egg noodles
1/2 cup finely chopped fresh parsley

Combine chicken broth and chicken in heavy large pot. Bring to boil. Reduce heat; cover partially and simmer until chicken is cooked through, about 20 minutes. Using tongs, transfer chicken to large bowl. Cool chicken and broth slightly. Discard skin and bones from chicken. Cut chicken meat into bite-size pieces and reserve.

Spoon fat off top of chicken broth and return to simmer. Add onion, carrots and celery. Simmer until vegetables soften, about 8-10 minutes.

Melt 2 tablespoons butter in heavy large skillet over medium-high heat. Add mushrooms and sauté until beginning to brown, about 5 minutes. Stir in lemon juice. Add mushrooms to broth; stir in noodles, parsley and reserved chicken. Simmer until noodles are tender, about 5 minutes. Season soup to taste with salt and pepper.

# Potato Leek Soup

2 large leeks, both the white and pale green parts,
  split lengthwise, washed well, and chopped
1 Tbsp unsalted butter
1-1/2 cups water
1 cup chicken broth
1 lb boiling potatoes, peeled and cut into 1/2-inch dice
2 Tbsp minced fresh parsley leaves
Salt and pepper to taste

In a large, heavy, covered saucepan over moderately low heat, cook the leeks in
the butter, stirring occasionally, for 8 to 10 minutes, or until they are softened
but not browned. Add the water, the broth, and the potatoes and simmer the
mixture, covered, for 20 minutes, or until the potatoes are tender. In a blender,
puree 1 cup of the soup; stir the puree into the remaining soup with the parsley,
and season the soup with salt and pepper.

# San Francisco Egg Drop Soup

6 cups chicken broth or clear soup stock
1/4 cup water
2 Tbsp cornstarch
2 eggs, beaten lightly
2 scallions, chopped

Mix cornstarch with water to form a paste. Bring soup stock to a boil. Slowly
pour in the cornstarch mixture while stirring the stock, until stock thickens.
Reduce heat and when soup is just simmering, pour the eggs in slowly, stirring
the soup at the same time. Shut off heat immediately and serve with chopped
scallions on top.

# Grandma Viareggio's Minestrone Soup

6 slices cooked ham, chopped
1/2 cup chopped onion
1 clove garlic, minced
1 28-oz can tomato sauce
5 cups water
2 cups thinly sliced cabbage
1 cup sliced zucchini, quartered
1 cup frozen green beans, thawed
1/2 cup thinly sliced carrots
Salt to taste
2/3 cup (4 oz) macaroni or alphabet noodles, uncooked

In large saucepan over medium heat, cook bacon until slightly browned; add onion and garlic. Cook 4 minutes or until tender.

Stir in remaining ingredients except pasta; heat to boiling. Reduce heat; simmer 30–40 minutes, covered, or until vegetables are tender.

Meanwhile, cook pasta according to package directions; drain. Stir pasta into soup; serve immediately. Makes 5 large bowls.

# Main Dishes

# Mediterranean Chicken with Artichokes

1-1/2 lbs boneless chicken breasts
1 Tbsp olive oil
1 large onion, sliced
2 cloves garlic, minced
1/4 cup white wine
1 16-oz can chopped tomatoes
1 4-oz can tomato paste
1 8-oz can artichoke hearts, drained and cut up
1/4 tsp oregano
1/4 tsp rosemary
1/4 tsp basil

In a large skillet, brown chicken in olive oil on both sides. Remove chicken and set aside. In the same skillet, sauté onion and garlic until tender. Add wine and stir. Return chicken to skillet, and add tomatoes, tomato paste, olives and herbs. Cover and simmer 20–25 minutes or until chicken is thoroughly cooked. Serve with rice or pasta.

# Chicken and Biscuit Casserole

2 cups cooked, cubed chicken
10 oz cooked broccoli
1 8-oz can cream of chicken soup
1/4 cup chopped onion
1/4 cup sour cream
1-1/2 tsp Worcestershire sauce
dash curry
1/2 cup grated Cheddar cheese
8-oz package refrigerated biscuits

Topping:
1/4 cup sour cream
1 egg
1 tsp celery seed
1/2 tsp salt

*This was a dish April Miller's nana made for her mother and now she makes it for her own children—it's a family favorite.*

Preheat oven to 375° F. Combine all ingredients except Cheddar cheese and biscuits in 1-1/2 quart casserole. Mix well. Bake for 20-25 minutes or until hot and bubbly. Sprinkle casserole with cheese. Cut biscuits into halves and arrange in casserole. Mix sour cream, egg, celery seed and salt to make topping; sprinkle over casserole. Return to oven and continue baking 25–30 minutes or until golden brown.

# Stuffed Chicken Breasts

4 boneless, skinless chicken breast halves (about 1-1/2 lbs)
4 oz mozzarella cheese, cut into 4 equal slices
3 Tbsp drained and chopped oil-packed sun-dried tomatoes
1/4 cup flour
2 Tbsp olive oil
2 cloves garlic, finely chopped
1/4 tsp oregano
1/4 tsp dried parsley
Salt and pepper to taste

Make 2 inch-long deep cuts in the center of each chicken breast to form pocket. Evenly stuff pockets with cheese and sun-dried tomatoes. Secure with wooden toothpicks. Sprinkle with herbs and salt and pepper. On a flat dish or board, dip chicken breasts in flour.

In a large skillet, heat oil over medium-high heat and brown chicken. Add garlic and cook, stirring, for 30 seconds. Cook covered for 6 minutes or until chicken is no longer pink.

# Roast Turkey with Herbes de Provence

10-lb turkey, at room temperature
1 lemon
3 stalks celery
2 medium onions
1 tsp salt
2 cloves garlic
3 sprigs parsley
4 tsp herbes de Provence
2 Tbsp olive oil
2 cups boiling water

Preheat oven to 325°F. Wash and dry turkey inside and outside. Cut lemon in half and rub inside of bird with one of the halves, squeezing out juice as you rub. Place both lemon halves inside turkey. Cut a celery stalk into 1" pieces and quarter 1 onion. Combine with salt, garlic, parsley, and 2 tsp herbes de Provence. Place mixture inside bird. Sprinkle half the remaining herbes in the neck opening. Truss by tying the wings close to the body and legs together. Rub the outside of the turkey with the olive oil and remaining herbs. Lay turkey, breast side down, on a rack and set in roasting pan. Slice remaining celery and onion and add to pan. Add boiling water. Bake 30 minutes. Turn turkey on its side, baste with pan juices, and bake 45 minutes. Turn on its other side, baste and bake 30 minutes more. Turn turkey breast side up, baste and bake for another 45–60 minutes, basting once or twice more. To test for doneness, insert an instant-read thermometer in the thickest part of the thigh, without touching bone. The thermometer should register 180°F. Transfer turkey to a hot platter, cover loosely with foil, and let rest at least 15 minutes before carving.

Prepare stuffing of your choice and serve with turkey.

We never set a table for fewer than 18 when my grandmother made Thanksgiving dinner. My favorite dish was really the Triple Cranberry Sauce (see p.54) and I could never get enough, but the prettiest thing on the table was the beautifully browned turkey, served on a platter with stuffing and surrounded by fresh cranberries.
    —Gloria Delaney

# North Dakota Meat Loaf

1–1 1/2 lbs ground beef (lean)
1–2 cups. soft bread crumbs
1 6–8 oz can tomato sauce
1 egg, beaten
4 Tbsp minced onion
3/4-1 tsp salt
1/8 tsp pepper
1/4 tsp dried sage

Preheat oven to 350°F. Beat egg in large bowl, add remaining ingredients and mix thoroughly, but do not overwork the mixture. Pack into 5 x 9 loaf pan. Bake for 60–70 minutes. If desired, spread with ketchup during last 10–15 minutes of baking.

# Salisbury Steak

1 lb ground beef
1/3 cup dry bread crumbs
1/2 tsp salt
1/4 tsp pepper
1 egg
1 large onion, sliced and separated into rings
1 8-oz can condensed beef broth
3 cups sliced mushrooms (about 1/2 lb)
2 Tbsp cold water
2 tsp cornstarch

Mix beef, bread crumbs, salt, pepper and egg. Shape into 4 oval patties, each about 3/4-inch thick. Cook patties in 10-inch skillet over medium heat about 10 minutes, turning occasionally until brown. Drain the skillet. Add onion, broth and mushrooms. Heat to boiling. Reduce heat, cover, and simmer about 10 minutes or until beef is done. Remove patties and keep warm. Heat onion mixture to boiling. Mix water and cornstarch; stir into onion mixture. Boil and stir 1 minute and serve over patties.

# Grandma Hitty's Flank Steak Roulade

*Hitty Linden from Cedar Falls, Iowa, made this wonderful dish for a dinner party in 1973 and still serves it.*

1-1/2 lbs lean flank steak
1/2 lb fresh spinach
3 cloves garlic, chopped
1 tbsp olive oil
2/3 cup sun-dried tomatoes
1/2 lb mozzarella cheese
1 tsp salt
Pepper to taste
1/4 cup Parmesan cheese

Preheat oven to 350°F. Butterfly flank steak and pound it flat with a meat mallot.

In a pot, wilt the fresh spinach leaves with the oil and garlic over low heat, and drain off the excess liquid. Set aside to cool. Soften sun-dried tomatoes in some hot water and set aside to cool.

Season the surface of the steak with garlic, salt, and pepper. On each steak place a layer of spinach, then the tomatoes, and last the mozzarella, leaving a border around the edges of the steak. Sprinkle with Parmesan cheese. Roll up each steak jellyroll-style and tie with butchers' twine to keep the steaks rolled.

Brown the steaks in a pan and then bake in a 350°F oven until cooked all the way through. Slice into roulades to serve.

# Hearty Pot Roast with Vegetables

2 lbs chuck round or rump roast
2 large cloves garlic, cut in slivers
1 tsp salt
1 tsp pepper
1/4 cup olive oil
2 onions, finely chopped
3 carrots, finely chopped
1 stalk celery, finely chopped

2/3 cup beef broth
1 28-oz can tomatoes in puree
1/2 tsp rosemary
1/2 tsp dill
2 bay leaves, crushed
2 cups baby carrots, peeled
4 potatoes, peeled and cut into large chunks
2 onions, cut lengthwise in quarters

Make small slits in meat and insert garlic slivers. Sprinkle meat with salt and pepper. In an ovenproof casserole, heat olive oil and then add meat and brown on all sides. Remove meat and set aside. Add chopped vegetables and cook on low heat for 10 minutes, stirring occasionally. Add beef broth and tomatoes and bring to a boil.

    Return meat to casserole dish and cover. Cook for 2 hours covered over low heat or until meat is very tender. Stir occasionally. Add baby carrots, potatoes, and onions, and simmer until vegetables are tender, about 30 minutes. Serve beef sliced on a serving platter surrounded by vegetables with sauce spooned over all.

# Shepherd's Pie

6–8 potatoes, mashed
1 lb ground beef
1 medium onion, chopped
2 slices bread
1 egg
2 garlic cloves, chopped

salt and pepper to taste
1/4 cup mustard
1/2 cup ketchup
1 cup frozen corn
1 cup frozen peas

Preheat oven to 350°F. In a skillet, brown beef well; drain. In large bowl, combine beef, bread, onion, egg, garlic, mustard, ketchup, salt and pepper. Mix thoroughly. Pat into bottom of greased casserole dish. Cover with peas and corn. Spread mashed potatoes on top. Cook covered about 30 minutes; uncover and cook an additional few minutes until potatoes are browned slightly.

# Spaghetti and Meatballs

1 8-oz package spaghetti
1/2 lb ground beef
1 egg
1-1/2 slices white bread, torn into small pieces
2 Tbsp grated Parmesan cheese
1/4 cup olive oil
1 8-oz can crushed tomato sauce
1 4-oz can tomato paste
1 tsp dried parsley
1 tsp dried oregano
Pinch dried dill
Salt and pepper to taste

Combine ground beef, egg, white bread, and Parmesan cheese in medium bowl. Season with salt and pepper. Heat oil in large, heavy skillet over medium-high heat. Form mixture into 1-1/2 inch-diameter meatballs. Cook meatballs until brown on all sides, about 8 to 10 minutes.

In a small saucepan over low heat, combined tomatoes, tomato paste, and herbs. Stir and cooked to desired thickness. Cook spaghetti according to package directions. Drain and top with meatballs and sauce.

# Garlic Lamb Chops

12 baby lamb chops
1 cup olive oil
1/2 cup freshly squeezed lemon juice
2 Tbsp chopped garlic
2 Tbsp chopped fresh rosemary (or 1 tsp dried rosemary)
Salt and pepper to taste

Quickly rinse the lamb chops under cold running water and pat dry with paper toweling. Place chops in a shallow bowl. Pour the oil and lemon juice over the lamb and sprinkle with the garlic and rosemary. Cover and marinate at room temperature for about 1 hour.

Prepare boiler. Remove the lamb from marinade and pat dry with paper toweling. Sprinkle with salt and pepper to taste. Place the lamb chops on the rack and cook, turning once, until done to preference, about 3 minutes on each side for medium-rare.

# Garden-Style Pork Chops

8 boneless pork chops, trimmed
1 large red pepper, diced
1 medium onion, thinly sliced
2 cloves garlic, minced
2 Tbsp olive oil
1 24-oz can chopped tomatoes
1 4-oz can tomato paste
1/2 tsp dried basil

In a large skillet, sauté red pepper, onion, and garlic in olive oil; remove and set aside. Thoroughly brown pork chops on both sides; drain fat. Return peppers to skillet. Add sauce and basil, and cover. Simmer about 45 minutes or until thoroughly cooked.

# Roast Loin of Pork with Cider Glaze

1 3-lb boneless pork loin, trimmed of fat
2/3 cup boiled cider or concentrated apple flavoring
4 large garlic cloves, minced
2 tsp dried ginger
2 tsp crumbled dried rosemary
1/2 tsp salt
2 Tbsp lemon juice
4 Tbsp oil
1/2 cup white wine
1 cup water

Preheat oven to 500°F. Place pork in small roasting pan. In a small bowl combine remaining ingredients, except wine and water. Rub mixture over pork, cover, and marinate for 30 minutes. Pour off and reserve cider mixture. Add wine to pan and place in oven. Roast 15 minutes. Reduce heat to 350 F and roast about 30 minutes, basting occasionally with cider mixture. Roast is done when thermometer registers 150°F. Remove from oven, transfer to carving board and let pork rest for 10 minutes. Place pan over medium heat. Add wine and water and scrape up caramelized bits, stirring until reduced slightly. Slice pork, add sauce, and serve immediately.

# Glazed Baked Ham

*According to Fran DeKalb, whose grandmother was a fine cook, a good ham does not need a complicated sauce.*

1 6–8-pound fully cooked boneless ham
Whole cloves if desired
1/4 cup honey
1/2 tsp dried mustard
1/4 tsp ground cloves

Preheat oven to 325°F. Place ham on rack in shallow roasting pan. Roast 12 to 16 minutes per pound.

Remove ham from oven. Pour drippings from pan. Cut surface of ham lightly in uniform pattern. Insert whole cloves if desired.

Mix honey, mustard, and ground cloves. Brush onto ham and roast uncovered about 20 minutes longer. Cover ham with tent of aluminum foil and let stand about 10 minutes.

# Chef Salad

1/2 head of romaine lettuce, rinsed, spun dry, and chopped fine (about 4 cups)
1/2 head of Boston lettuce, rinsed, spun dry, and chopped fine
   (about 4 cups)
1/2 bunch of watercress, coarse stems discarded and the watercress rinsed,
   spun dry, and chopped fine (about 2 cups)
1/2 lb ham steak, cooked and diced
1/2 lb Cheddar cheese, diced
2 whole skinless boneless turkey or chicken breasts (about 1 1/2 pounds total),
   cooked, and diced
2 tomatoes, cut up
3 hard-boiled eggs, cut up
1/3 cup red-wine vinegar
1 Tbsp Dijon-style mustard
2/3 cup olive oil
Salt and pepper to taste

In a large salad bowl toss together the romaine and the Boston lettuce, and the watercress. Add the chicken, ham, and cheese. In a small bowl whisk together the vinegar, the mustard, and salt and pepper to taste, add the oil in a slow stream, whisking, and continue until the dressing is emulsified. Pour it over the salad, and toss. Decorate the top with eggs and tomatoes.

# Glazed Grilled Salmon

2 7- or 8-oz salmon steaks, about 1/2-inch thick
3 Tbsp dark brown sugar
4 tsp Dijon-style mustard
1 Tbsp soy sauce
1 tsp rice wine vinegar

In a medium bowl, combine brown sugar, mustard and soy sauce. Whisk to blend. Transfer 1 Tbsp glaze to small bowl and add rice vinegar; set aside.

　Brush 1 side of salmon steaks with half the glaze in the medium bowl. Place salmon steaks, glazed side down, in broiler. Grill until glaze is slightly charred, about 4 minutes. Turn salmon over and brush with remaining glaze. Grill about 5 minutes, until second side of salmon is slightly charred and salmon is just opaque in the center. Transfer salmon to plates and drizzle reserved glaze from small bowl over salmon and serve.

# Shrimp Scampi

3 large cloves garlic, minced
7 Tbsp olive oil
1-1/2 lbs large shrimp, peeled and deveined
1/4 cup dry white wine
2 tsp lemon juice
2 tsp minced parsley
1/4 tsp oregano
Salt and pepper to taste

In a large skillet, lightly sauté garlic in oil. Add shrimp and sauté until just pink, about 3 minutes. Add wine, lemon juice, parsley, oregano, salt and pepper. Simmer until heated through.

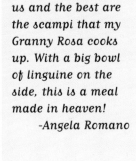

*Shrimp is a treat for us and the best are the scampi that my Granny Rosa cooks up. With a big bowl of linguine on the side, this is a meal made in heaven!*
*-Angela Romano*

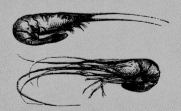

# Sole with Lemon Cream Sauce

2 lbs sole fillets (or any other white fish such as flounder,
   whiting or fluke), cut into 4 pieces
2 Tbsp butter
1/4 cup flour
3/4 cup heavy cream
Grated zest of 1/2 lemon
1 Tbsp lemon juice
2 Tbsp chopped fresh parsley (or 1 tsp dried parsley)
Salt and pepper to taste

In a large frying pan, melt the butter over moderate heat. Sprinkle the fish with salt and pepper. In a shallow bowl or dish, dip the fish into the flour and shake off any excess. Cook the sole for 2 minutes. Turn over and cook about 2 minutes longer, or until fish is just done. Remove sole from pan.

   Add the cream and lemon zest to pan. Simmer and cook until the sauce begins to thicken, about 2 minutes. Stir in the lemon juice, parsley, and salt and pepper to taste. Serve the sauce over the fish.

# Tuna Noodle Casserole with Mushrooms

*This is a perfect Grandpa recipe for those very rare occasions when Grandma has the flu.*

9 Tbsp butter (1 stick + 1 Tbsp)
1/4 cup flour
2-1/2 cups whole milk
1-1/2 cups sliced mushrooms
1/2 cup scallions
1/4 cup chopped celery

1 tsp dried rosemary
1 tsp dried thyme
1 8-oz package egg noodles
1 12-1/2-oz can tuna packed in water, drained well
1-1/2 cups fresh white breadcrumbs
Salt and pepper to taste

Preheat oven to 350°F. Butter an 8-inch square glass baking dish.

Melt 4 Tbsp butter in medium saucepan over medium heat. Add flour and stir 2 minutes. Gradually whisk in milk and stir over medium heat until sauce thickens, about 5 minutes. Remove from heat.

In medium skillet over medium-high heat, melt 1 Tbsp butter. Add mushrooms, scallions, and celery. Sauté until mushrooms are tender, about 5 minutes. Stir in rosemary and thyme. Stir mushroom mixture into sauce.

Cook noodles in large pot of boiling salted water until tender but firm. Drain and rinse under cold water.

Place tuna in large bowl. Using a fork, flake tuna into bite-size pieces. Add noodles and sauce and toss to coat. Season with salt and pepper. Transfer mixture to prepared baking dish.

In a skillet, melt remaining butter. Add breadcrumbs and stir until golden brown. Sprinkle breadcrumbs over casserole and bake until casserole bubbles around the edges, about 30 minutes.

# Paella

3 cups rice washed
5 cups chicken broth
3 medium onions, finely sliced
6 Tbsp olive oil
3 large ripe tomatoes, chopped
10 cloves of garlic, minced
1 tsp paprika
1/2 tsp saffron
1 lb chicken breast, cut into 1-inch strips

1 lb firm fish (scrod, haddock)
  cut up into 1–2 inch pieces
1 lb medium shrimp, peeled and
  deveined
1/2 lb scallops
1 cup sliced mushrooms
2 red peppers, cut up
1/2 cup white wine
1 Tbsp Tabasco sauce

Simmer the rice in the chicken broth under a cover until it is just tender, about 20 minutes. Remove from heat and let sit.

In a skillet, sauté the onion in 3 Tbsp of oil for 2–3 minutes. Add tomatoes, garlic, saffron and paprika, and simmer for 20 minutes.

In a separate skillet, heat the rest of the oil and sauté the chicken for a minute. Add the fish, shrimp, mushrooms and peppers and sauté for 3 or 4 minutes, stirring gently so fish does not break up.

Put the rice, the tomato mixture, sauted fish and vegetables into a large pot. Add the scallops on top and stir them in gently. Add the wine and Tabasco. Cook covered on very low heat for 20 to 30 minutes. You can also preheat the oven to 400°F and bake the paella in the oven for 30 minutes.

# Virginia Crab Cakes

2 cups diced crab meat (about 3/4 lb)
1 cup fresh bread crumbs
2 large eggs
1/2 cup heavy cream
Dash hot sauce (to taste)
2 tsp Worcestershire sauce
2 tsp chopped fresh parsley leaves
2 tsp grated onion
2 Tbsp butter

In a bowl, combine crab meat and bread crumbs. In a small bowl, whisk eggs
well and add cream. Add the cream mixture to the crab. Add hot sauce
Worcestershire sauce, parsley, onion, salt and pepper to the crab mixture and
combine well.

   In a large heavy skillet, heat 1 Tbsp butter over moderate heat until foam
subsides. Drop crab mixture into the skillet by tablespoons. Cook crab cakes
until  golden brown, about 2 minutes on each side. Continue cooking crab cakes,
adding butter to the pan as needed. Serve crab cakes warm.

# Greek Pasta Salad with Tomatoes and Olives

2 cups cooked pasta, such as rigatoni or penne,
   drained and cooled
8 cherry tomatoes, sliced in half
1 sliced onion
1/2 sliced cucumber
12 black pitted olives
Olive oil to taste
1 cup diced feta cheese
Oregano to taste
Salt and pepper to taste

Mix pasta, vegetables, olives, and cheese together in a large bowl. Pour the oil over them and mix. Sprinkle some salt, pepper, and oregano on top.

# Stuffed Shells

1 16-oz box jumbo shells
4 cups ricotta cheese
12 oz mozzarella cheese, shredded
3/4 cup grated Parmesan cheese
2 eggs, slightly beaten
Dash garlic powder
1 tsp dried oregano
1 tsp dried parsley
1 20-oz jar tomato sauce

Preheat oven to 350°F. Cook shells according to directions. Drain in cold water to stop cooking.

Mix together ricotta cheese, mozzarella cheese, 1/2 cup Parmesan cheese, eggs, and garlic powder. Crush the dried herbs in the palms of your hands and stir into the cheese mixture. Stuff shells with cheese mixture.

Spread 1/3 of spaghetti sauce in the bottom of a 15 x 10 baking pan. Place shells, open side up, close together in the pan. Spread remaining sauce on top and sprinkle with remaining Parmesan cheese. Bake for 25–35 minutes, or until bubbly. Let stand 10 minutes before serving.

# Zucchini and Spinach Frittata

*Sometimes when Grandma and I spend the day at the mall in New Jersey, trying on clothes and shoes in every store, we're too tired to cook a big dinner. That's when Grandma makes her special zucchini and spinach frittata. We call it our "heavy duty shopper's special."*

*-Donna Ruggiero*

6 Tbsp olive oil
1/2 lb zucchini, cut into 1/4-inch dice
1 large bunch spinach, washed well,
  spun dry, and chopped coarsely
10 large eggs
1-1/2 tsp dried tarragon, crumbled
Salt and pepper to taste

In a large non-stick skillet, heat 2 Tbsp oil over moderately high heat and sauté zucchini until it begins to brown. Add spinach and cook, stirring occasionally until just wilted. Season with salt and pepper. Remove skillet from heat and cool vegetables slightly.

Preheat oven to 225°F. Grease a large baking sheet.

Beat eggs lightly in a large bowl. Stir in vegetables, tarragon, and salt and pepper to taste. In a 9-inch heavy omelet pan heat 1 Tbsp oil over moderately low heat until not but no smoking, and add 1 cup egg mixture, tilting pan to distribute evenly. Cook egg mixture until set underneath but still slightly wet in center, about 3–4 minutes. Slide frittata half out of pan onto prepared baking sheet and fold second half over to make a half circle. Keep frittata warm in oven. Using the same technique, make 3 more frittata with remaining oil and egg mixture. Keep frittata warm until ready to serve. Cut each frittata into 3 wedges.

# Side Dishes and Salads

# Sweet Potato Pie

3 large sweet potatoes
2 egg yolks
1/4 tsp nutmeg
Dash salt
2 Tbsp brown sugar
8-inch prepared pie crust

Preheat oven to 400°F. Boil sweet potatoes until tender. Peel and mash. Add egg yolks, nutmeg, salt, and brown sugar. Beat mixture until it is creamy. Turn into pie crust and bake until crust browns, about 20-25 minutes

# Pan-Roasted Potatoes

2 lbs small red-skinned potatoes
4 Tbsp (1/2-stick) butter
Salt and pepper to taste
Parsley for garnish

Wash potatoes and peel if desired. (Most cooks leave the flavorful thin skins on the potatoes.) Heat butter in large skillet over medium heat. Add potatoes; lower heat and cover. Sauté, adjusting heat as needed, stirring occasionally, until tender. Serve immediately.

# Creamy Mashed Potatoes

8–10 small, all-purpose potatoes (white or russet), peeled and cut into 2-inch cubes
1 stalk celery, including leaves
1 bay leaf
1 large clove garlic
4 Tbsp (1/2-stick) butter, chopped into small pieces
1/4 cup heavy cream
1/2 tsp salt
Pepper to taste

Place potatoes in a large cooking pot. Add enough
cold water to barely cover potatoes. Add whole
celery stick, garlic clove and bay leaf. Bring to a boil and then simmer,
covered, for 20–30 minutes, or until potatoes are tender. Pour off liquid,
reserving about a third of it for mashing. Discard celery, garlic and bay leaf.

   Using the same pot, add the butter and cream to the potatoes. Mash by
hand or whip with an electric mixer. As you mix, add as much of the hot
reserved cooking liquid as necessary to achieve desired consistency.

# Basic Bread Stuffing

1/4 lb (1 stick) butter
1/2 cup finely chopped scallions or onions
4 cups (approximately) fresh bread crumbs, crusts and all
1/2 Tbsp fresh tarragon or 1 tsp dried tarragon
1/2 cup finely chopped parsley
Salt and freshly ground black pepper to taste
1 cup chicken broth

Place the butter and scallions or onions in a saucepan, and allow the butter to
melt over low heat. Lightly sauté the shallots. Combine with the crumbs and
other ingredients and toss lightly. Add chicken broth and cook until the stuffing
is the way you like it. Add more melted butter if needed, and taste for seasoning. Serve warm.

   For a variation, you can substitute 1/2 tsp dried thyme, 1/4 (or less) tsp dried
sage, 1 tsp summer savory, or 1 tsp dried basil. You can also add chopped
pecans, chopped walnuts, or 1 cup finely diced celery to the stuffing. Adjust
the quantities of bread and/or liquid to reach desired consistency.

# Buttercup Squash

1 medium buttercup squash
4 Tbsp (1/2 stick) butter
Salt to taste

Nutmeg to taste
1/4 cup maple syrup
2 large Granny Smith apples, sliced

Preheat the oven to 350°F and butter a casserole dish. Spread the apple slices around the bottom of the casserole.

Cut buttercup squash—unpeeled—into 8 pieces and steam until the inside is soft but shells remains somewhat firm. When squash meat is slightly cooled, scoop out into a bowl and mash. Whip the mashed squash with 1/4 cup butter, salt and nutmeg to taste, and maple syrup.

Place apples in a casserole dish. Spoon the squash over apple slices. Bake in casserole for 10 to 15 minutes. Serve warm.

# Sweet Noodle Pudding

1 16-oz package broad noodles,
  cooked and drained
1-1/2 pints sour cream
1-1/2 cups melted butter
1-1/2 cups sugar

1 tsp vanilla
5 eggs, beaten
1 cup raisins
1 Tbsp cinnamon mixed with
  2 Tbsp sugar

Preheat oven to 350°F. Grease 9 x 13-inch pan. Combine all ingredients except cinnamon-sugar mixture. Pour into prepared pan. Sprinkle cinnamon-sugar on the top and bake for 45 minutes.

# Boston Baked Beans

2 cups Great Northern beans, or small dried white beans, soaked overnight
2 tsp dry mustard
3 Tbsp dark brown sugar
3 Tbsp molasses
1/4 lb salt pork, cut into 1/2-inch cubes with rind attached

Preheat oven to 325°F. Drain the beans, cover with fresh water, and cook until tender, about 1 hour. Drain, reserving the liquid. Stir together the mustard, brown sugar, molasses and 2 cups of reserved liquid. Place salt pork in 2-quart casserole, add the beans and the molasses mixture. Stir to blend. Cover and bake for 5–6 hours. They are done when soft. Check every hour or so to make sure the beans don't dry out. Add more of the reserved liquid as needed to keep the beans moist.

# Corn Pudding

1 8-oz can creamed corn
2 eggs, beaten until frothy
2 Tbsp flour
1/4 cup melted butter
1/2 cup milk
1/4 cup sugar
1/4 tsp salt

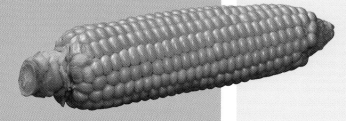

Preheat oven to 350°F. Butter a 2-quart casserole. Combine all ingredients in a large bowl and pour into Prepared casserole. Bake for 1–1-1/2 hours.

# Tomato Onion Bake

4 cups sliced tomato
2 cups diced or grated onion
Salt and pepper to taste

Pinch sugar
1 cup soft bread crumbs
2 Tbsp butter

Preheat oven to 350°F. Filled greased oven-proof dish with layers of tomato, onion, salt, pepper, and a little sugar. Sprinkle bread crumbs on top. Continue layering and finish top with bread crumbs. Dot with butter. Bake for about 35 minutes or until cooked.

# Roasted Asparagus with Lemon

3 Tbsp fresh lemon juice
1 Tbsp olive oil
1 tsp finely grated lemon peel
36 asparagus spears, trimmed
Salt and pepper to taste

Preheat oven to 450°F. Mix lemon juice, oil, and lemon peel in 15 x 10 x 2-inch baking dish. Add asparagus; turn to coat. Sprinkle with salt and pepper. Roast asparagus until crisp-tender, turning occasionally, about 20 minutes. Serve warm or at room temperature.

# Ratatouille

3 Tbsp virgin olive oil
2 cups chopped onions
2 1-lb eggplants, unpeeled and cut into
   1-inch cubes
4 garlic cloves, minced
2 zucchini, cut into 1-inch pieces
1 red pepper, cut into 1-inch pieces
1 yellow pepper, cut into 1-inch pieces
6 cups (about 2-3/4 lbs) seeded, coarsley chopped ripe tomatoes
2 tsp thyme or 3 fresh thyme sprigs
1 tsp rosemary or 1 fresh rosemary sprig
1 bay leaf
4 Tbsp dried basil or 1/4 cup minced fresh basil

In a large heavy pot, heat oil over medium heat. Add onions and sauté until tender, about 10 minutes. Add eggplants and garlic and sauté 5 minutes. Add zucchini and peppers and continue sautéeing another 5 minutes. Add tomatoes and herbs and stir to mix. Cover, reduce heat to medium-low and cook until vegetables are tender and flavors have blended, about 40 minutes, stirring occasionally. Discard bay leaf and stir in basil. Season with salt and pepper and transfer to serving dish. Can be served hot, warm or cold

# Creamed Spinach

2 10-oz packages frozen spinach
6 bacon strips
1 garlic clove, minced
1/2 cup chopped onion
1/2 tsp salt
1/8 tsp white pepper
1 pinch cayenne pepper
2 Tbsp butter
2 Tbsp flour
1 cup half-and-half or whole milk

Prepare spinach by boiling or in microwave.
Drain well and squeeze out as much moisture as possible. Chop fine, using food processor or food grinder.
    Cook bacon in skillet until crisp. Remove and
drain. Crumble and set aside. Pour off all but a little
of the bacon fat from the skillet; sauté garlic and onion
over medium heat. When onion is limp, add spinach. Lower heat. Season with
salt, white pepper and cayenne; stir well as moisture evaporates from spinach,
about 1 minute. Remove from heat.
    In a separate large skillet, melt butter over medium heat. Sprinkle in flour,
stirring constantly until smooth. Gradually stir in half-and-half or milk and cook
until smooth and bubbly. Stir in spinach mixture and heat through. Remove from
heat, stir in reserved bits of bacon, and serve.

# Orange Rice

2 cups uncooked regular long grain rice
1 Tbsp + 1 tsp grated orange peel
1 tsp ground nutmeg
4 cups sliced carrots
4 cups hot chicken broth
1/2 cup orange juice
1/2 cup chopped parsley

Preheat oven to 350°F. In ungreased 3-quart casserole, mix rice, orange peel
and nutmeg. Stir in carrots and broth. Cover and bake 30–35 minutes until liquid
is absorbed Sprinkle with orange juice. Add parsley and toss until well mixed.
Let stand 5 minutes before serving.

# Spinach Salad

1/2 cup virgin olive oil
1/2 onion, cut into 1-inch chunks
1/4 cup red wine vinegar
1 teaspoon Worcestershire sauce
1 teaspoon dry mustard
4 bacon slices
1 bunch spinach, washed, trimmed,
  torn into bite-size pieces
6 mushrooms, sliced
2 hard-boiled eggs, chopped
1/2 cup croutons

Purée first 5 ingredients in blender or food processor until smooth and emulsified. Set dressing aside.

Cook bacon in heavy medium skillet over medium heat until crisp. Drain bacon on paper towels. Crumble. Combine spinach and remaining ingredients in large bowl. Add enough dressing to season to taste. Toss well. Garnish salad with bacon and serve.

# Lentil Salad with Balsamic Vinaigrette

1 thick slice of red onion
1 cup chopped red onion
3 fresh parsley sprigs + 1/2 cup
  chopped fresh parsley
2 garlic cloves, minced
1 cup dried brown lentils
2 tablespoons olive oil
3 tablespoons balsamic vinegar
2 teaspoons Dijon mustard
Salt and pepper to taste

Bring medium saucepan of water to boil. Add onion slice, 3 parsley sprigs and 1 minced garlic clove and bring to boil. Stir in lentils. Reduce heat and simmer uncovered until lentils are just tender, about 20 minutes. Drain. Discard onion and parsley sprigs.

Stir oil, vinegar, mustard and remaining garlic in small saucepan over low heat until just warm (do not boil). Place warm lentils in bowl. Add chopped onion, chopped parsley and warm vinaigrette; toss to coat. Season with salt and pepper. Serve warm or at room temperature.

# Blue Cheese Salad Dressing

1 large garlic clove, minced and mashed
   to a paste with 1/4 teaspoon salt
1 Tbsp Dijon mustard
2 Tbsp fresh lemon juice
2 Tbsp white wine vinegar

1/3 cup olive oil
1/3 cup sour cream
3/4 cup crumbled blue cheese
   (about 3 ounces)
Salt and pepper to taste

In a blender or small food processor blend together the garlic paste, mustard, lemon juice, vinegar, and salt and pepper to taste. With the motor running add the oil and blend the mixture until it is combined well. Add the sour cream, 3/4 cup of the cheese, and 2 tablespoons water (or enough to obtain the desired consistency). Blend the dressing until it is combined well, and transfer it to a bowl. Stir in additional crumbled blue cheese if desired. Makes about 1-1/3 cups and keeps, covered and chilled, for about 1 week.

# Italian Salad Dressing

6 Tbsp olive oil
2 Tbsp white wine vinegar
2 Tbsp chopped fresh parsley or
  2 tsp dried parsley
1 Tbsp fresh lemon juice

2 garlic cloves, chopped
1 tsp dried basil, crumbled
1/4 tsp dried crushed red pepper
Pinch of dried oregano
Salt and pepper to taste

Combine all ingredients in small bowl and whisk to blend. Season to taste with salt and pepper. Makes about 1/2 cup. (Can be prepared 1 day ahead and kept chilled.)

# Barbecue Sauce

1/2 cup chopped onion
1/2 cup cider vinegar
2 8-oz cans tomato soup
2 8-oz bottles ketchup

2 Tbsp unsalted butter
3 Tbsp Worcestershire sauce
Salt, pepper, and sugar to taste

Combine all ingredients and simmer for 30 minutes. Store in refrigerator for
up to 1 week. Can be frozen. Makes 1 quart.

# Triple-Cranberry Sauce

1 cup frozen cranberry juice cocktail
    concentrate, thawed
1/3 cup sugar
1 12-ounce package fresh or frozen
    cranberries, rinsed, drained

1/2 cup dried cranberries (about 2 ounces)
3 tablespoons orange marmalade
2 tablespoons fresh orange juice
2 teaspoons minced orange peel
1/4 teaspoon ground allspice

Combine cranberry juice concentrate and sugar in heavy medium saucepan.
Bring to boil over high heat, stirring until sugar dissolves. Add fresh and dried
cranberries and cook until dried berries begin to soften and fresh berries begin
to pop, stirring often, about 7 minutes. Remove from heat and stir in orange
marmalade, orange juice, orange peel and allspice. Cool completely. Cover; chill
until cold, about 2 hours. (Can be made 3 days ahead. Keep refrigerated.) Makes
about 2-1/2 cups.

# Fried Apple Rings

4 Tbsp (1/2-stick) butter
2 medium-large firm apples, cored and
    sliced into 1/4 or 1/2-inch rings
5 Tbsp sugar
2 tsp cinnamon

Melt the butter in a large skillet over medium heat. Place
about half the apple rings in a single layer in the skillet. Mix
together the sugar and cinnamon and sprinkle half over the apple rings.
Cook for 2 minutes and then turn the apple rings over and reduce the
heat to very low. Cover the skillet and cook for 2–4 minutes more. Repeat
with remainder of apple rings. Serve warm.

# Desserts

# Phoebe's Pound Cake

1/2 cup shortening
1 cup butter
2 1/2 cups white sugar
5 eggs

2 teaspoons flavoring (vanilla, almond,
    lemon, or other)
1 cup milk
1/2 teaspoon baking powder
3 cups flour

Preheat oven to 300°F. Lightly grease and flour one 9- or 10-inch loaf pan.
Cream shortening, butter, and sugar until light and fluffy (for best
results use an electric mixer). This will take a while. Add eggs one
at a time, beating well after each addition. Beat in flavoring.
Combine baking powder and flour. Alternately stir
in flour mixture with milk into creamed mixture,
starting and ending with flour. Pour batter into
prepared pan. Bake for 1 to 1-1/2 hours or until
a cake tester comes out clean. Serve plain or
with strawberries and whipped cream.

# Pecan Squares

Crust:
2/3 cup confectioner's sugar
2 cup unbleached all-purpose flour
1/2 lb (2 sticks) sweet butter, softened

Topping:
2/3 cup (approx. 1-1/3 sticks) melted
    sweet butter
1/2 cup honey
3 Tbsp heavy cream
1/2 cup brown sugar
3-1/2 cups shelled pecans,
    coarsely chopped

Preheat oven to 350°F. Grease a 9 x 12 inch baking pan.

Sift sugar and flour together. Cut in butter, using 2 knives or a pastry blender
until fine crumbs form. Pat crust into the prepared baking pan. Bake for 20 minutes; remove from oven.

Mix melted butter, honey, cream and brown sugar together. Stir in pecans,
coating them thoroughly. Spread over crust. Return to oven and bake for 25
minutes more. Cool completely before cutting into squares.

# Black Forest Cherry Cake

1 egg, slightly beaten
1-2/3 cups sugar
1-1/2 cups milk
3 1-oz squares unsweetened baking
  chocolate, cut up
1-3/4 cups flour
1 tsp baking soda
1/2 tsp salt
1/2 cup shortening

1 tsp vanilla
2 eggs
1 pint whipped cream

Filling:
1 16-oz can pitted dark sweet cherries
4 tsp cornstarch
1/4 cup cherry Kirsch if desired

Preheat oven to 350°F. Grease and lightly flour 2 9-1/2 inch round cake pans.

In a saucepan, combine beaten egg, 2/3 cup sugar, 1/2 cup milk, and chocolate. Cook and stir until mixture just boils. Cool. Combine flour, baking soda and salt in a mixing bowl.

In a large bowl, beat in the shortening for 30 seconds; add remaining 1 cup sugar and vanilla, and beat until fluffy. Add the 2 eggs, beating after each. Add dry ingredients and remaining 1 cup milk alternately to mixture, beating after each addition. Stir in chocolate mixture and pour into baking pans. Bake for 25–30 minutes. Cool 10 minutes and remove cake from pans and continue to cool.

Drain cherries, reserving 1/2 cup liquid. Heat liquid with cornstarch and mix. Add cherries, the kirsch if desired, and heat until bubbly. Allow to cool. To assemble, place 1 cake layer on a serving plate, spread with cherry filling and whipped cream. Place second layer on top and cover with whipped cream.

*Grandmother Hugendorf's Black Forest Cherry Cake is so famous that no one lets her come visit unless she brings it with her. It's so good that you wish they would let you skip dinner and go straight to dessert!*

# Carrot Cake

1-1/2 cups vegetable oil
2 cups sugar
4 eggs
2 cups flour
2 tsp baking soda
1 tsp salt
3 tsp cinnamon
2 tsp vanilla
3 cups grated carrots

Icing:
1/4 lb (1 stick) margarine          1 pkg confectioner's sugar
8 oz cream cheese                    2 tsp vanilla

Preheat oven to 325°F.

Combine oil and sugar; add eggs. Sift together flour, soda, salt and cinnamon. Add to sugar mix and beat well. Add vanilla and grated carrots.

Bake in 2 well-greased 8-inch layer cake pans for 45 minutes.

Soften margarine and cream cheese and beat together. Add confectioners' sugar and vanilla and stir until spreading consistency. Spread icing over each layer of carrot cake and on top.

# Elegant Poached Pears

2 small firm-ripe Bosc or Bartlett pears (about 6 ounces each)
2 cups cranberry-raspberry juice cocktail
1/2 cup sugar
2 bay leaves
2 whole cloves
1 tsp julienne orange zest

Core pears from bottom ends with melon-ball scoop and peel, leaving tops and stems intact.

In a 2-quart saucepan simmer pears in juice with remaining ingredients, uncovered, turning occasionally, 10–15 minutes, or until pears are tender but still hold their shape. Transfer pears to a plate with a slotted spoon, reserving poaching liquid, and chill in freezer 15 minutes.

While pears are chilling, boil reserved liquid until reduced to about 1 cup. Remove bay leaf and cloves. Pour liquid into a bowl and put bowl in a larger bowl of ice and cold water. Stir liquid until cooled lightly.

Serve pears in shallow bowls with some poaching liquid.

# All-American Apple Pie

1/3 cup light brown sugar
1/3 cup white sugar
1 Tbsp flour
1 tsp lemon juice
1/3 tsp ground cinnamon

7-1/2 cups peeled and pared Rome
   (or other) apples (about 2-1/2 lbs)
1 cup raisins
pie dough for doublecrust pie
1 egg, beaten

Preheat oven to 425°F Spray deep dish pie plate with cooking spray. In a large bowl, combine white sugar, light brown sugar, flour, lemon, and cinnamon and mix well. Add apples and raisins to sugar mixture. Stir until fruit is well coated.

Place pie crust into pie plate. Spoon apple mixture into pie shell. Place second crust on top of filling, and trim edges. Lightly glaze top of pie with a beaten egg, then sprinkle with a little sugar. Bake until golden brown, about 35–40 minutes. Place on a wire rack, and cool 30 minutes.

# Grammy Wendy's Christmas Cookies

3/4 lb butter (3 sticks), softened
2-1/4 cups sugar
1 egg
1 tsp nutmeg

1/2 tsp baking soda
1 cup milk
10 cups (or less) all-purpose
   unbleached flour

Cream the butter and sugar in a large bowl. Add the egg and beat well. Beat in the nutmeg. Dissolve the baking soda in the milk, and add to creamed mixture, alternating with flour. Start with half the flour and gradually add more until dough is the consistency you like for rolling. Chill dough in several batches. When well chilled, remove from the refrigerator, one batch at a time.

Preheat oven to 375°F. Dough may need to soften slightly before rolling. Roll to thickness of about 1/4 inch. Cut out with large cookie cutters. Place on greased cooking sheets and bake for approximately 10 minutes. Remove from cookie sheets and cool before eating.

*These are very heavy cookies, perfect for "dunking." Grammy Wendy made these every year and divided them into tins for each of her grandchildren. My daughters and I have continued this favorite Christmas tradition.*

   *-Helen Jenkins*

# Peach Cobbler

8 cups sliced fresh peaches
2 cups sugar
2–4 Tbsp flour
1/2 tsp ground nutmeg
1 tsp vanilla
1/3 cup butter
Pastry for double crust pie

Preheat oven to 475°F. Combine peaches, sugar, flour and nutmeg in saucepan. Set aside until syrup forms. Then bring peaches to a boil, reduce heat to low and simmer for about 10 minutes or until tender. Add vanilla and butter, stirring until butter melts.

Roll half of pastry dough into an 8-inch crust. In an 8-inch baking pan, spoon half the peach mixture and place pastry layer on top. Bake for 10 minutes until lightly brown. Roll out remaining pastry and cut into strips. Pour remaining peach mixture on top of first crust and criss-cross pastry strips on top of peaches. Bake for 15–18 minutes until lightly browned.

# Strawberry Buttermilk Biscuit Shortcake

7 cups fresh strawberries, washed, hulled, and halved
   (or quartered if very large), approximately 2 1-pound baskets
1/2 cup + 3 Tbsp sugar
2 Tbsp raspberry preserves
1 cup chilled whipping cream
1 tsp vanilla extract
1 package buttermilk biscuits
Powdered sugar

Combine strawberries, 1/2 cup sugar and raspberry preserves in large bowl;
toss to coat. Let stand until syrup forms, tossing occasionally, about 1 hour.

Beat chilled whipping cream, vanilla extract and remaining 3 tablespoons
sugar in another large bowl until stiff peaks form. Cover and chill.

Meanwhile, bake buttermilk biscuits according to package directions. Cool
and cut biscuits in half. Place each biscuit bottom in dish or shallow bowl. Top
each generously with strawberries and whipped cream. Cover fruit and cream
with biscuit tops. Dust biscuits with powdered sugar and serve.

*This was my Grandpa Willy's favorite treat. Especially wonderful was serving this on the Fourth of July on a blue plate.*
                                          *-Flo Ridgewood*

# Mud Pie

1 cup granulated sugar
1/4 lb (1 stick) butter, melted
1/3 cup flour
1/3 cup baking cocoa
1 tsp vanilla
1/4 tsp salt
2 eggs
1 cup chopped nuts, if desired
1/4 cup hot fudge sauce or topping
1 cup whipping (heavy) cream
2 Tbsp confectioners' sugar
Readymade single pie crust

Preheat oven to 325°F. Grease bottom and side of 8 x 1-1/2 inch round pan, or 9-inch pie plate.

In a medium bowl, stir together sugar, butter, flour, cocoa, vanilla, salt and eggs. Stir in nuts. Pour into pan.

Bake 25–30 minutes or until edge appears dry and toothpick inserted halfway between center and edge comes out clean (center will be moist). Immediately prick holes in pie with toothpick. Spread 1/4 cup fudge sauce over top. Cool completely.

Beat whipping cream and confectioners' sugar in chilled medium bowl with electric mixer on high speed until stiff. Spread around top of pie. Cover and refrigerate any remaining pie.

# Lemon Squares

1 cup flour
1/4 lb (1 stick) butter, softened
1/4 cup powdered sugar
1 cup sugar
2 tsp grated lemon peel

2 tbsp lemon juice
1/2 tsp baking powder
1/4 tsp salt
2 eggs
Confectioners' sugar for top

Heat oven to 350°F. Mix flour, butter and 1/4 cup powdered sugar. Press into ungreased 8 x 8 x 2 square pan, building up to 1/2-inch high. Bake 20 minutes or until crust is done.

Beat sugar, lemon peel, lemon juice, baking powder, salt and eggs with mixer on high speed about 3 minutes or until light and fluffy. Pour over hot crust. Bake for 25–30 minutes or until center bounces back from touch. Cool. Dust with powdered sugar. Cut into 1-1/2-inch squares.

# Rice Pudding

3 cups milk
2 Tbsp cornstarch
1/3 cup sugar
1/2 cup long grain rice, uncooked
1/2 tsp cinnamon
1/4 cup raisins
1 tsp vanilla
Cinnamon sticks for garnish

In a large saucepan, combine milk, cornstarch, and sugar. Bring to a slow boil, stirring constantly. Add rice. Cook until thick, stirring well. Remove from heat. Stir in remaining ingredients. Cool slightly if serving warm, otherwise cover and chill. Garnish with cinnamon stick.

# Chocolate Chip Cheesecake

2 8-oz packages cream cheese, softened
1/2 cup sugar
1/2 tsp vanilla
2 eggs
3/4 cup miniature semi-sweet chocolate chips
1 9-oz prepared graham cracker crust

Preheat oven to 350°F. Mix cream cheese, sugar and vanilla with electric mixer on medium speed until blended. Add eggs and mix. Stir in 1/2 cup of the chocolate chips. Pour mixture into crust and sprinkle the top with remaining chocolate chips.

   Bake for 40 minutes or until center is almost set. Cool. Refrigerate 3 hours or overnight.

# Lemon Meringue Pie

1 14-oz can sweetened condensed milk
2 egg yolks
1/2 cup fresh squeezed lemon juice
3 egg whites
4 1/2 teaspoons white sugar
1 teaspoon vanilla extract
1 graham cracker crust

Preheat oven to 350°F.

Beat egg yolks, and combine with milk; mix very well. While beating egg mixture, pour in lemon juice. Mix well. Pour lemon mixture into graham cracker crust.

In another bowl, beat egg whites until soft peaks form. Gradually beat in sugar, and continue beating egg whites until stiff peaks form. Spoon meringue on pie.

Bake approximately 8–12 minutes until golden brown. Cool. Refrigerate until ready to serve.

# Key Lime Pie

1 cup graham cracker crumbs
3 Tbsp sugar
4–5 Tbsp melted butter
1/2 cup key lime juice (or enough lemons and key limes to get 1/4 cup of juice from each.
3 eggs

Pinch cream of tartar
Pinch salt
1 14-oz can sweetened condensed milk
1 cup whipping cream
1 lime

Preheat oven to 325°F. Mix graham cracker crumbs with sugar and melted butter. Press into 9 inch pie plate and bake for 5 minutes. Remove from oven and let cool.

Separate 2 of the eggs, placing the two egg whites into a mixing bowl. In another bowl, reserve the yolks, add one whole egg, 1/2 cup juice, and sweetened condensed milk. Mix well.

With clean mixer blades, beat the egg whites until stiff, but not dry, adding salt and cream of tartar after about 20 seconds. Fold whites into filling mixture. Pour filling into partially baked crust. Bake 10-15 minutes or until set. Let cool at room temperature, then freeze 4 hours to overnight.

Just before serving, whip cream to form stiff peaks. Serve decorated with whipped cream and lime slices.